Tammy Graves Publishing

Copyright © 2016

POSITIONED TO LIVE

Tammy Graves

(Workbook)

Copyright © 2015 by Tammy Graves
Tammy Graves Publishing
Houston Texas
ISBN- 13: 978-0692771341
ISBN- 10: 0692771344
Unless otherwise indicated, Scripture verses are taken from the NKJV, KJV, NLT and ESV. ©

All rights reserved. No parts of this publication may be reproduced, stored in a retrieval system, or transmitted in any form without prior permission of the publisher and or author. Printed in the United States of America

ABOUT THE AUTHOR

Tammy Graves is the founder and Pastor of Oasis Outreach Ministries and is also an Occupational Safety Specialist with Tennessee OSHA. She holds a Master of Business Administration degree from Union University, a Bachelor of Science degree from Middle Tennessee State University and an Associate of Science degree in Pre-Med from Jackson State Community College. Ms. Graves attended Memphis Bible Institute and served her country for six years in the United States Army Reserves. She has been a guest speaker at numerous seminars, conferences, and summits. She enjoys freelance writing, reading, public speaking, teaching, running, cooking and traveling. She's also a certified personal trainer. Ms. Graves is a resident of Jackson, Tennessee.

ACKNOWLEDGEMENTS

This book was conceived in 2007. The Lord kept saying wait; it is not time. He began to impart more revelation and insight over the years. This year He said, "Now is the appointed time"; nine years later. I thank God for His timing and for knowing what His people need and when they need it. I dedicate this book to the most important person in my life – Jesus. Lord Jesus, you are the love of my soul. Thank you for choosing me and for my position in your Kingdom. I hope that I have pleased you.

I thank my spiritual father and mentor, Bishop Elroy Hicks, for seeing who I am when I could not. I thank you for your patience, compassion and love. Thank you for being to me and for me what others forfeited. I love you Bishop.

I thank Prophetess Margaret White, for being my Samuel and my Nathan when the wilderness seemed endless. Your love has been unconditional and has strengthened me through my make over. I love you Mother.

I thank Dorinda Myles, for being unselfish and pouring into me in the time of famine. Your trust and friendship has been a breath of fresh air. I love you my true friend.

INTRODUCTION

"You weren't born just to live a life and to die; you were born to accomplish something specifically." — Dr. Myles Munroe

> *The Spirit of the Lord is upon me,*
> *Because he hath anointed me*
> *To preach the gospel to the poor;*
> *He hath sent me to heal the brokenhearted,*
> *To preach deliverance to the captives*
> *And recovering of sight to the blind,*
> *To set at liberty them that are bruised;*
> *To preach the acceptable year of the Lord.*
> *— Luke 4:18-19*

21 DAY INSIGHT AND DIRECTION FAST
(Scriptures: New Living Bible Translation)

"We have fasted before you they say. Why aren't you impressed? Why don't you see or sacrifices? Why don't you hear our prayers? We have done much penance, and you don't even notice it. I'll tell you why! Because you are living in evil pleasure even while you are fasting, and you keep right on oppressing your workers.

Look, what good is fasting when you keep on fighting and quarreling? This kind of fasting will never get you anywhere with me. Is this what I want – this doing of penance and bowing like reeds in the wind and putting on sackcloth and covering yourselves with ashes? Is this what you call fasting? No, the kind of fast I want is that you stop oppressing those who work for you and treat them fairly and give them what they earn. I want you to share your food with the hungry and bring right into your homes those who are helpless, poor and destitute. Clothe those who are cold and don't hide from relatives who need your help. If you do these things, God will shed his own glorious light upon you. He will heal you; your godliness will lead you forward, and goodness will be a shield before you, and the glory of the Lord will protect you from behind. Then, when you call, the Lord will answer. Yes, I am here, he will quickly reply.

All you need to do is stop oppressing the weak, and to stop making false accusations and spreading vicious rumors! Feed the hungry! Help those in trouble! Then your light will shine out from the darkness, and the darkness around you shall be as bright as day. And the Lord will guide you continually, and satisfy you with all good things, and keep you healthy too; and you will be like a well-watered garden, like an ever flowing spring" (Isaiah 58:3-11, LB).

Fast in Hebrew is *tsom* and *nesteia* in Greek. It means voluntary abstinence from food. Fasting comes from the Hebrew word *tsum*, which is the practice of self-denial. For the next 21 days you will be denying yourself food that provides pleasure to your flesh. You must dedicate yourself to this fast by committing your mind, body, soul and spirit to the directions of the Holy Spirit. First, you have to prepare your body to fast. Three days prior to the fast, you should eat light foods such as soup, salads, green vegetables, broths, Jell-O, and drink plenty of water; to reduce the possibility of constipation. You should not eat meat that takes at least three days to digest such as beef. During this fast you should choose a time that will accommodate your lifestyle. For instance, if you work a 9 to 5 job, you might consider this time as your fast time.

You might consider spending 30 minutes to an hour before leaving for work, in prayer and studying the word. Then on your breaks, instead of eating, meditate on the scriptures assigned to each day in this workbook/journal. When you return home, pray 30 minutes to an hour before eating dinner. When you eat dinner, do not eat or drink any pleasure foods such as bread, desserts, sodas, tea, coffee, wine, beef, pork, etc. I suggest you eat salads, vegetables, chicken, fish, fruits, nuts and drink plenty water. I also recommend that you drink water only and drink it throughout the day; especially if you are not accustomed to fasting.

If you have never fasted or if you have never fasted in this manner or for this length of time, I suggest you start out skipping one of the three meals for the first week and build up if you can. However you decide, remember no pleasure foods. Your body is going to crave the foods you have subjected to it. It will go through withdrawal. Fight it! If you deny it, around day 3 to day 5, it will get over it! It will submit! Keep in mind you are making a commitment to God and that you have a purpose and a goal; which is to gain direction and insight as it pertains to what God is desiring you to do and where to go (relocate) spiritually as well as naturally; in this season of your life.

During leisure time, instead of engaging on/in social media, study and meditate in/on the word. Please be mindful and seek your doctor before starting a fast if you are on medications.

YOU GOT THIS! LET'S FAST!

POSITIONED TO LIVE

Chapter 1-4 Questionnaire

1. No man can nor will ever have as many positions in the Kingdom of God as_____.

2. We have been placed on the earth with a _____ and a Kingdom assignment.

3. What did Jesus say to Mary at the wedding reception in Cana?_____.

4. How do you make the presence your permanent residence?_____.

5. Where was the presence of God (The Ark of the Covenant)?

6. Who watched over the Ark of the Covenant?

   _____.

7. Where did the Philistines take the Ark of the Covenant?

8. David's set time as king manifests; revealing his

   _____.

9. The Body of Christ must give God an _____ willingly with its heart.

10. He empowers us to do the greater works and; we will accomplish them if we allow

    _____

11. What are some of the reasons some ministries never advance to the next level?-

    _____

12. We must prepare our _____ while traveling on our assigned path.

13. God is eternal and His anointing is _____.

14. What year did the Lord visit the author as she was asleep? Was it Winter, Spring, Summer or Fall?
_____.

15. How many troops did David gather, when we went to Baal Judah? _____.

16. By touching the Ark of the Covenant, Uzza made God _____.

17. Why would God kill a man for touching the Ark of the Covenant?
_____

18. What did God tell Moses to tell his chosen people to build?_____.

19. God tells them to count all males from the age of _____ who were able to work in the Tabernacle.

20. Why do you believe the Church is experiencing the spiritual death of Uzza — a separation from the presence of God?

_____

_____

21. What did God tell Moses and Aaron, who were positioned by God as leaders? _____

22. Aaron's rod represents?

_____.

23. Today's leaders have become legalistic and_____.

24. Why is God supernaturally resetting the dislocation of The Body of Christ?

25. Give a brief summary of Chapter Four and how it relates to your position in The Body of Chirst.-

_____
_____
_____
_____
_____
_____
_____
_____
_____
_____
_____
_____
_____

Chapter 5-7 Questionnaire

1. What Chapter in the Bible did Jesus hear of John the Baptist's murder?

2. Jesus is moved with_____and begins to minister to them.

3. How was the grain separated from the straw and husk in Uzza's days?
   _____

4. he threshing floor is the place on the other side where your position and assignment is tread upon repeatedly to separate_____ _____

5. What question did the author suggest that you wait until you read the last word of the book to answer? _____.

6. What is God trying to do with your mind?_____.

7. God wants you to allow Him to break the cycle of the system's mindsets that are built up in you. What are these systems?

_____

_____

8. What are the stages of our natural and physical growth and development?

_____

How does that relate to our Spiritual growth?_____

9. What does Isaiah 43:18-20 mean to you personally?

_____

_____

_____

_____

10. What are the different spiritual locations and different levels of anointing? _____
_____
_____
_____
_____
_____

11. Is the anointing transferable? _____

12. After being under Elijah's mentorship and leadership for ten years, what did Elisha experience?
_____
_____
_____
_____
_____

13. What does the word Gilgal mean?
_____.

14. Everyone has to go through_____to reach the Jordan; the most prosperous place on the other side.

15. You cannot walk in the double portion anointing without a_____.

16. Joshua was instructed by God to remain where?
_____.

17. As you enter into Gilgal you will notice that your _____ changes.

18. How many years did Elisha serve Elijah?
_____.

19. Where did Prophet Samuel anoint Saul as King of Gilgal?
   _____.

20. What does the word Bethel mean?
   _____.

21. Why did God tell Abraham to relocate?
   _____
   _____

22. What does the word Ur mean?
   _____.

23. How does Abraham assignment relate to the assignment on your life?
   _____
   _____
   _____
   _____
   _____

_____

_____

24. What chapter in Genesis did Jacob relocate to Beersheba?

_____

25. What does the word Jericho means?

_____

26. Before you move into the spiritual location of Jericho, something has to _____

27. In Jericho, the Lord teaches you how to tame your _____; how to use the weapon of_____.

28. What does the word Jordan means?

_____.

29. Now, you are "**Positioned to**_____" You have been baptized in the_____ and the spirit of God has_____ down upon you.

Day 1

But if we confess our sins to him, he can be depended on to forgive us and to cleanse us from every wrong. (1 John 1:9)
Yes, ask anything using my name and I will do it. (John 14:14)
Heavenly Father, I repent for all my sins. I ask you to cleanse me of all unrighteousness according to 1 John 1:9 and John 14:14. I receive my forgiveness now. To God be the Glory. In Jesus name Amen.

Today: Mediate on letting God have complete, total control of everything in your life. He has even forgiven you this day for trying to live your life in your power and your strength and for not using the name of Jesus when you ask for help.

Journal your feelings, thoughts, emotions (including hunger pains)

Journal: What did the Holy Spirit speak to you today (Remember He speaks in different ways: (i.e., your spirit, an audible voice, another person, nature, song, billboard, while studying the word of God)

_____
_____
_____
_____
_____
_____
_____
_____

Day 2

This plan of mine is not what you would work out, neither are my thoughts the same as yours. For just as the heavens are higher than the earth so are my ways higher than yours and my thoughts than yours. (Isaiah 55:8-9)

Heavenly Father, I come to you today in the name of Jesus. I renew and give my total allegiance to you. This is a fresh new day; a new beginning for me and my relationship with you. I commit myself to you. Father, I submit my will to your will. I present my life as a living sacrifice, unto you which is my reasonable service. Transform me into your image daily my Father. In Jesus name Amen.

Today: Mediate on the thoughts of Love God thinks toward you. He has given you His son Jesus to believe on so that you could have an everlasting life. And your everlasting life begins here on earth. Your everlasting life has a direction and a destiny he wants to position you into.

Journal: How do you feeling about where you are now and the direction you feel God is leading you in. (If you do know where He is leading you there will be a clearer understanding by the end this fast).

_____
_____
_____
_____
_____
_____

Day 3

For a shepherd comes through the gate. The gatekeeper opens the door for him and the sheep hear his voice and come to him; and he calls his own sheep by name and leads them out. (John 10:3)

Heavenly Father, I am your sheep. I ask you to teach me to hear your voice distinctly, clearly. Increase your anointing on me to clearly hear and know your voice and not that of a stranger. Give me the ability to recognize you when you speak and give me the patience to listen to you. In Jesus name Amen.

Today: Mediate on how a shepherd watches over the sheep and cares for their every need. He protects them and guides them to safety. Jesus is your shepherd and you do not have to be afraid. He is going to lead you into your divine destiny. He is going to help you reach your spiritual location in God, because a shepherd always positions the sheep to live.

Journal: How do you feeling about whether or not you trust that the Good Shepherd/Jesus is assigned to and is protecting you?

_____
_____
_____
_____
_____
_____
_____

Day 4

Life and death is in the power of the tongue. (Proverbs 18:21) Heavenly Father, I align my words with your words. Loose the power and effects of any word curses that I have spoken over my life and upon the life of others. I repent of having spoken those negative words about myself, my children, my family, my finances, my health, my friends and my relationship with you. I repent of known words and unbeknownst in anger. In Jesus name Amen.

Today: Mediate on the power of the Word of God and the importance of speaking and declaring what He says.

Journal: What Word has God given you today or in times past? Did it bring salvation, peace, joy, deliverance, relief, etc.?

_____
_____
_____
_____
_____
_____
_____

Day 5

Create in me a new, clean heart, O God, filled with clean thoughts and right desires. (Psalms 51:10)
Heavenly Father, You have created a clean heart in us; you have renewed a right spirit within us. You have made old things pass away and all things new. Thank you for not casting us away from your presence when we failed you. Thank you for your goodness and for new mercy every day that endures forever. In Jesus name Amen.

Today: Mediate on the importance of the right thoughts, the right ideas and the right motives. Focus on how your heart responds to righteousness.

Journal: How have your thoughts, ideas and motives have changed in the last 5 days?

_____
_____
_____
_____
_____
_____
_____

Day 6

Your words are a flashlight to light the path ahead of me, and keep me from stumbling. (Psalms 119:105)
Heavenly Father, I pray that my path is like the shining sun and not of darkness. Your word says the path of the just is like the shining sun that shines ever brighter unto a perfect day. Lead me each day into paths of righteousness for your name sake. Do not let me stumble and fall. In Jesus name Amen.

Today: Mediate on the times you stumbled and fell. And the Lord sent His word and picked you up and showed you the way.

Journal: What lessons have you learned in not following His path; walking in the light?

_____
_____
_____
_____
_____
_____
_____
_____

Day 7

So, dear brothers, you have no obligation whatever to your old sinful nature to do what it begs you to do. For if you keep on following it you are lost and will perish, but if through the power of the Holy Spirit you crush it and its evil deeds, you shall live. (Romans 8:12-13)

Heavenly Father, I crucify my flesh now. I die daily from self-desires and live to do your desires. I command my mind to shut up and stop reminding me of my faults, of my shortcoming and of my sins. There is no condemnation to me because I am in Christ Jesus. In Jesus name Amen.

Today: Meditate on the Forgiveness of God.

Journal: What has your flesh overcome so far during this fast?

_____
_____
_____
_____
_____
_____
_____

Day 8

They defeated him by the blood of the Lamb, and by their testimony; for they did not love their lives but laid them down for him. (Revelation 12:11)

Heavenly Father, Help me to accept that I am more than a conqueror through Christ Jesus. I am an overcomer. Thank you for strengthening me to overcome by the blood of Jesus and the word of my testimony. In Jesus name Amen.

Today: Meditate on the obstacles, trials, situations and circumstances you have overcome during this fast.

Journal: Your testimony.

Day 9

I pray that your hearts will be flooded with light so that you can see something of the future he has called you to share. I want you to realize that God has been made rich because we who are Christ's have been given to him. I pray that you will begin to understand how incredibly great his power is to help those who believe him. (Ephesians 1:18-19)

Heavenly Father, I ask that you give me knowledge of your will in all wisdom and spiritual understanding and the strength and might of you. Help me to know and to understand what is my hope and calling in Christ Jesus. I want to do what you say do, go where you say go and be who you called me to be. In Jesus name Amen.

Today: Meditate on how wise God is and your need for His wisdom in all things.

Journal: What areas do you need wisdom in? What areas have you received wisdom in since starting this fast?

_____
_____
_____
_____
_____
_____
_____

Day 10

Not by might nor by power, but by my Spirit says the Lord. (Zechariah 4:6)
Heavenly Father, Help me not to be moved by what I see or hear. Help me not to be moved by reason. Help me to be moved by your Spirit and your Word only. Help me to cease from my own labors. I do so by faith. In Jesus name Amen.

Today: Meditate on how the Holy Spirit desires to move and will move on your behalf.

Journal: What is the Holy Spirit doing in you, around you and through you since this fast?

_____
_____
_____
_____
_____
_____
_____

Day 11

Oh, that you would wonderfully bless me and help me in my work; please be with me in all I do and keep me from evil and disaster. (1Chronicles 4:10)
Heavenly Father, Position me to live. Enlarge my territory, increase my borders. Expand my thinking and help me to write the vision so that I may run with it. Let me see where you desire for me to be in this season of my life. Lend me your eyes Holy Spirit and show me what is and what is to come. In Jesus name Amen.

Today: Meditate on the vision/revelation that the Lord has given you.

Journal: Write the vision/revelation.

_____
_____
_____
_____
_____
_____
_____

Day 12

If you want favor with both God and man, and a reputation for good judgment and common sense, then trust the Lord completely; don't' ever trust yourself. (Proverbs 3:5)
Heavenly Father, your word tells me to trust you with all my heart. Help me to trust you. Help my unbelief. I no longer want to be wise in my own eyes. Jesus, I confess you as my Lord, my Savior, my Deliverer and my Redeemer. Thank you for strengthening my heart and for encouraging me this day. In Jesus name Amen.

Today: Meditate on the thing(s) you still have not surrendered to God.

Journal: What you are going to finally Let Go and Let God Have?

_____
_____
_____
_____
_____
_____
_____

Day 13

For whatever God says to us is full of living power: it is sharper than the sharpest dagger, cutting swift and deep into our innermost thoughts and desires with all parts, exposing us for what we really are. (Hebrews 4:12)

Heavenly Father, your word is alive and active. It is sharper than any double-edged sword. Your word says you shall decide and decree a thing and it shall be established for you and the light of your favor shall shine upon my way. Today I decide and decree what shall be established for me. In Jesus name Amen.

Today: Make your decrees. (i.e., I am the head and not the tail; I am above only and not beneath, I am healed, I am positioning myself to live)

Journal: Write your decrees and meditate on them.

_____
_____
_____
_____
_____
_____
_____
_____

Day 14

We live within the shadow of the Almighty, sheltered by the God who is above all gods. This I declare, that he alone is my refuge, my place of safety; he is my God and I am trusting him. (Psalms 91:1-2)

Heavenly Father, thank you for rescuing me from every trap set by Satan. For your word says he comes but for to steal, kill and destroy. Jesus has overcome him and I have been given the same authority and power. I rebuke him and his plots and plans assigned against me; for the weapons he has formed against me are not prospering. You are shielding me and hiding me under your mighty wings, Father. I am safe. In Jesus name Amen.

Today: Meditate on how it feels to be held close in a strong intimate embrace. Visualize God holding you in his arms.

Journal: How did the vision of the embrace made you feel?

_____
_____
_____
_____
_____
_____
_____
_____

Day 15

O God, my God! How I search for you! How I thirst for you in this parched and weary land where there is no water. How I long to find you! (Psalms 63:1)

Heavenly Father, I hunger and thirst after you. I desire your righteousness; I desire your glory. Fill me up Lord. Let my cup overflow. Make known your presence to me; that I might be positioned to live. I lift up my hands to you in prayer and bless you. Fully satisfy me O Lord. In Jesus name Amen.

Today: Mediate on what you desire most from the Lord.

Journal: Write your desire.

_____
_____
_____
_____
_____
_____
_____

Day 16

Be strong and brave, for you will be a successful leader of my people. (Joshua 1:1)

Heavenly Father, I rebuke the spirit of fear. You have not given me the spirit of fear but rather you have given me power, love and a sound mind. I have the mind of Christ Jesus. I am of good courage and you have strengthened my heart. Thank you. In Jesus name Amen.

Today: Mediate on the strength and direction(s) this fast has given you.

Journal: What are you no longer afraid of?

_____
_____
_____
_____
_____
_____
_____

Day 17

And the Lord came and called as before, Samuel! Samuel! And Samuel replied, Yes, I'm listening.
(1 Samuel 3:10)
Heavenly Father speak; I am listening. I long to hear your voice today. I await your instructions and your directions. I search for you with my whole heart. I am available to you my Lord. In Jesus name Amen.

Today: Meditate on what he spoke to you.

Journal: What did he speak to you?

_____
_____
_____
_____
_____
_____
_____

Day 18

Finishing is better than starting! (Ecclesiastes 7:8)
Heavenly Father, I thank you for giving me the strength to run the race set before me. Thank you for giving me the patience to endure hardship as a good soldier. I know that weeping has endured for a night but my morning of joy has come. In Jesus name Amen

Today: Meditate on how the joy of the Lord is your strength.

Journal: How you are feeling in your spirit today?

_____
_____
_____
_____
_____
_____
_____

Day 19

Listen to my prayer, O God; don't hide yourself when I cry to you. Hear me, Lord! Listen to me! For I groan and weep beneath my burden of woe. (Psalms 55:1)

Heavenly Father, I thank you for hearing my cry during this fast. Thank you for listening to me as I groaned and wept beneath my burden. Your anointing has destroyed the yoke and removed the burden. I casted my cares on you and you have delivered my soul. I praise you O Lord, my God. In Jesus name Amen.

Today: Meditate on the very moment you felt the burden lift.

Journal: How does it feel to be free?

_____
_____
_____
_____
_____
_____
_____

Day 20

This is the message God has given us to pass on to you: that God is light and in Him is no darkness at all. (1 John 1:5)
Heavenly Father, I thank you for being the Light of my life. Thank you for showing me the way that I must go. Thank you for leading me to you through this fast. All things have now become new. I thank you that you are doing a new thing and it is springing forth. Father, I recognize it. It has become clear. This is the dawning of a new day and a new season in my life. I accept your command for me to relocate spiritually. I vow to move to higher heights and deeper depths in you so that you might get the glory and men might see you in me and glorify you Jesus. In Jesus name Amen.

Today: Meditate on the new you and the move you are about to make.

Journal: How did this fast and this book change your life?

_____
_____
_____
_____
_____
_____
_____

Day 21

Arise, my people! Let your light shine for all nations to see! For the glory of the Lord is streaming from you. All nations will come to your light; mighty kings will come to see the glory of the Lord upon you. (Isaiah 60: 1; 3)

Heavenly Father, I thank you for waking me up from a deep sleep. I thank you for shaking me, for stirring my spirit and arousing me. I have received the due order of your will. I will carry the weight of your glory as I leave, Gilgal to travel to Bethel to travel to Jericho to make my abode in the promise land of Canaan. The land you promised that I shall possess. It is mine and everything in it. You are giving me my portion. You are not holding back any good thing from me. Lord, thank you that every good and perfect gift comes from you. You are exceeding my expectations Father. You will continue to do exceedingly abundantly above all that I have thought or asked of you. Father, your love and your presence have consumed me. I am in awe of you. I love you. In Jesus name Amen.

Today: Meditate on the direction you must now go in.

Journal: Who must you leave behind?

_____
_____
_____
_____
_____
_____
_____

www.ingramcontent.com/pod-product-compliance
Lightning Source LLC
LaVergne TN
LVHW051206080426
835508LV00021B/2828